COUNTRY LICKS
for Guitar

by
Steve Trovato
and Jerome Arnold

T0052792

PLAYBACK+
Speed • Pitch • Balance • Loop

To access audio visit:
www.halleonard.com/mylibrary

Enter Code
2321-4715-3821-7337

ISBN 978-0-634-01392-5

Visit Hal Leonard Online at
www.halleonard.com

Contact us:
Hal Leonard
7777 West Bluemound Road
Milwaukee, WI 53213
Email: info@halleonard.com

In Europe, contact:
Hal Leonard Europe Limited
42 Wigmore Street
Marylebone, London, W1U 2RN
Email: info@halleonardeurope.com

In Australia, contact:
Hal Leonard Australia Pty. Ltd.
4 Lentara Court
Cheltenham, Victoria, 3192 Australia
Email: info@halleonard.com.au

Introduction

As an art form, country music has been a constantly growing and ever-changing force in American music, while still retaining and nurturing the roots that gave it life. Similarly, country guitarists are a unique, versatile breed themselves, drawing from a wide range of musical influences that would astound not only the casual listener, but also other musicians. As an example, years before electronic gadgets became staples of rock 'n' roll, effects such as talk boxes, echo units, reverb, vibrato bars, wah-wah, octave dividers, and fuzz tones were used on country records.

The stage was set on August 1, 1927 in Bristol, Tennessee, when Jimmy Rodgers recorded his first sides for the Victor Company. Rodgers, originally from Mississippi, was heavily influenced by the black blues musicians he had met in his travels as a railroad brakeman. The most notable of these was Blind Blake, "The Father of Ragtime Blues," whose recording of "He's in the Jailhouse Now" predates the version from Rodgers by nearly two years.

In 1935, Bob Dunn, with Milton Brown's Musical Brownies, became the first electric steel guitarist to record. Dunn was noted for his ability to phrase like a big band horn section, not only on the jazz standards of the day, but on western and "hillbilly" tunes as well.

Jimmy Wyble played with Bob Wills' Texas Playboys and Spade Cooley in the late forties and early fifties. With both groups, he demonstrated a driving swing style (influenced by Charlie Christian) that later led to his positions with jazz greats Benny Goodman and Red Norvo. Today, Wyble is still very active and is garnering acclaim for his "classical jazz" style of contrapuntal improvisation.

During the fifties, Grady Martin and Hank Garland could not only be heard on country records, but they also played on rockabilly, rhythm 'n' blues, and rock sessions as well. Garland, who was one of the most highly regarded guitarists in Nashville, set the entire jazz community on its ear in 1961 with his bebop album *Jazz Winds from a New Direction*.

Chet Atkins, by 1960, had established himself as country music's leading guitar virtuoso. He also appeared at the Newport Jazz Festival and with symphony orchestras around the country. As one of the most influential guitarists of the twentieth century, Chet influenced the rockabilly styles of James Burton, Scotty Moore, Carl Perkins, and even a young rock player from Liverpool named George Harrison. Later, Chet was responsible for recording and producing his two most accomplished disciples: Jerry Reed, finger stylist deluxe; and Lenny Breau, one of the world's leading jazz guitarists.

On the west coast, at the same time, Jimmy Bryant was melting strings with his high-velocity country jazz, while bluegrass flatpicker extraordinaire Clarence White created a new vocabulary for the Tele, first with the prototypical country-rock band Nashville West and later with The Byrds.

The country guitarists mentioned above (and the many more who were not) have accounted for some of the most exciting and innovative playing in American music to date. In writing this book, we have tried to capture the essence of modern country guitar and its myriad influences. We hope that this volume will expand your current repertoire of musical ideas and help you develop a personal style of country guitar.

Table of Contents

Editor's Note: Due to the personal nature of the right-hand technique, picking directions are left to the preference of each player. Jerome plays with a thumbpick and fingers, while Steve usually plays with a combination of flatpick and fingers. As a rule of thumb (no pun intended), we offer this suggestion: Experiment, play slowly, and always use the easiest possible choice for right-hand picking.

Also, the accompanying audio will assist you in deciphering the fingering, sound, and timing of each lick. Each example is performed twice—once up to speed and once slowly.

Single-String Licks

◆ Pro Lick #1

Here's a very typical lick or tag in C. It lays well on the fingerboard and employs a unison bend in bar 2.

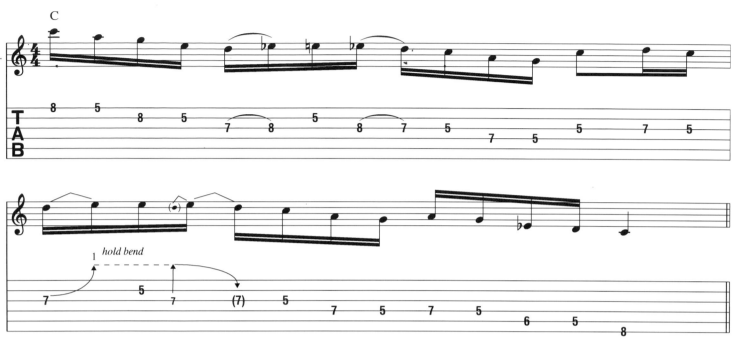

◆ Pro Lick #2

This dominant lick works great in country tunes as a V7 moving to the tonic. It also works well in swing tunes.

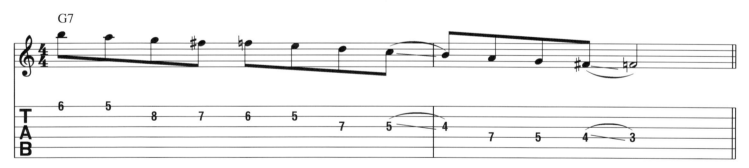

◆ Pro Lick #3

This lick works well over a C (I) or Am (vi). If you move it up a minor third, it will work over Cm or E♭. Remember, any tonic major lick moved up three frets will give you a tonic minor lick.

* meas. 2-3 repeat three times in fast version

◆ 4 ▷ Pro Lick #4

This is a familiar lick utilizing sixth intervals. Try playing all the notes on the third string with your pick, and all the notes on the first string with your middle finger.

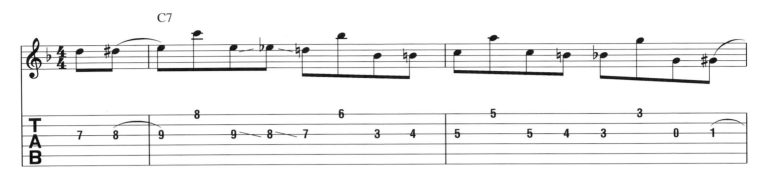

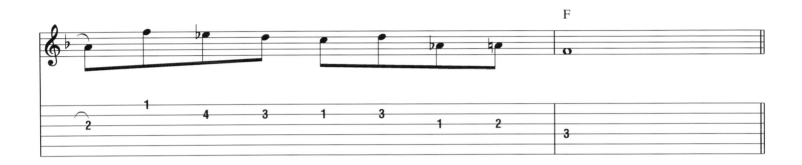

◆ 5 ▷ Pro Lick #5

This lick also works well over Am.

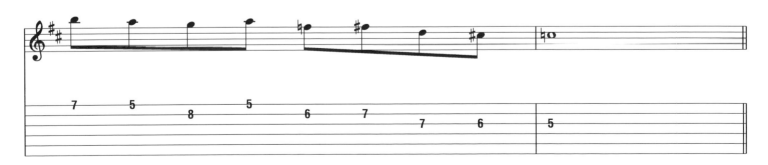

◆6 Pro Lick #6

This bluegrass flatpicking lick is written in open position (using open strings), but it should also be worked out in closed position (no open strings) so that it may be transposed to other keys.

◆7 Pro Lick #7

Here we have a very bluesy lick which uses unison bends in bars 1 and 2. I suggest shifting from fifth to second position at beat 3 of bar 2.

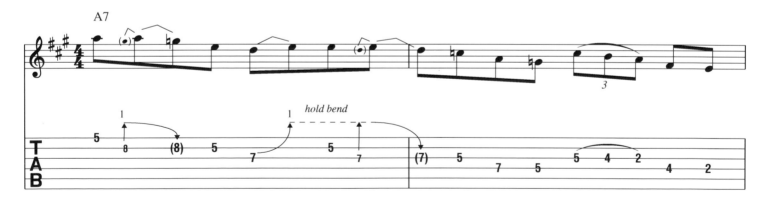

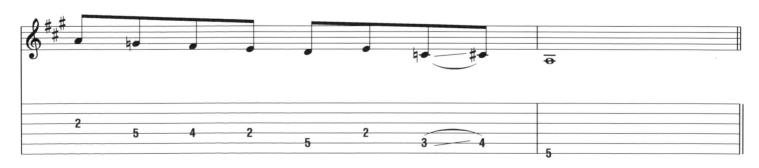

:➡ Pro Lick #8

The fourth note in this long two-octave single line in G is an open E string. As the lick is transposed to other keys, the open E can remain as part of the lick because it is passed over so rapidly.

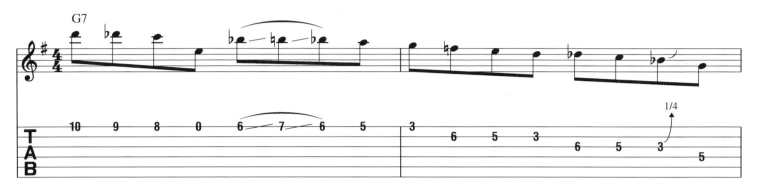

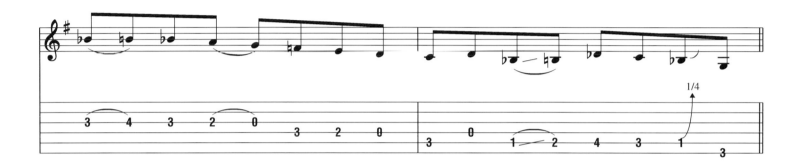

:➡ Pro Lick #9

This is a movable lick with a bluesy flavor. A position shift from fourth to ninth is required at bar 2. Note the upward sweep at the end of bar 3. This is done by sweeping the pick across strings 3, 4, and 5 using an upstroke.

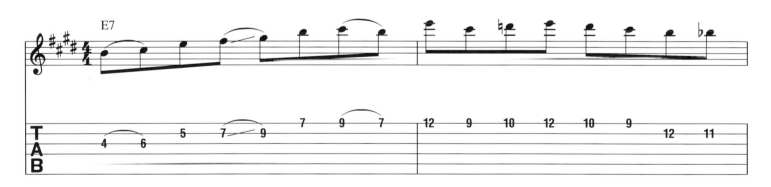

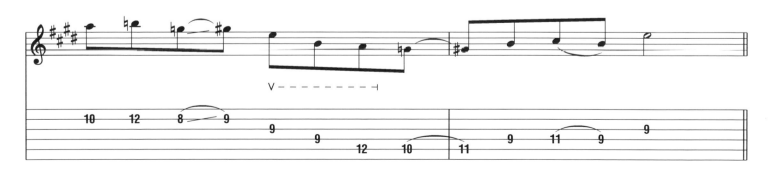

◆10 Pro Lick #10

This is a lick in the style of Albert Lee. Although it may look difficult, it's actually one of the easier ones. Any problems with phrasing will be cleared up by the audio. Bar 1 is merely a blues lick with an open B string interspersed throughout.

◆11 Pro Lick #11

The only trick here is to learn the lick slowly and remember that speed is the by-product of accuracy.

Pedal-Steel Licks

◆12◆ Pro Lick #12

This is a cliché pedal-steel lick. Notice that several times the B note is bent up to C# throughout the first two bars.

◆13◆ Pro Lick #13

This is a lengthy pedal steel-type lick over a fairly common country progression. In bar 1, the F is bent to F# and held to pitch throughout the bar. This happens again in bar 5. Bar 7 has some diffcult double-string bends, so be sure and listen to the audio to hear how they're suppose to sound.

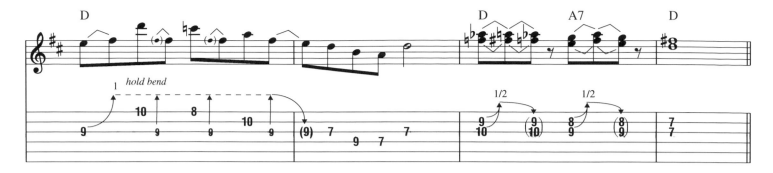

##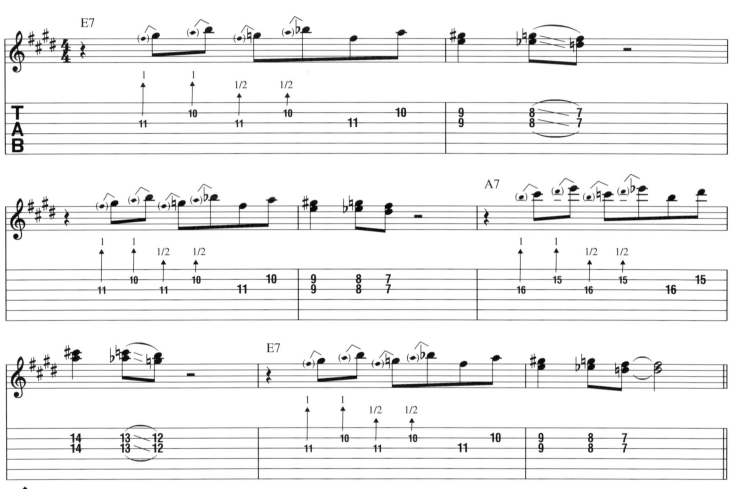

14 Pro Lick #14

Here is a typical country lick. Be careful with the two string bends; they are difficult to play in tune but absolutely necessary for that Hawaiian guitar flavor.

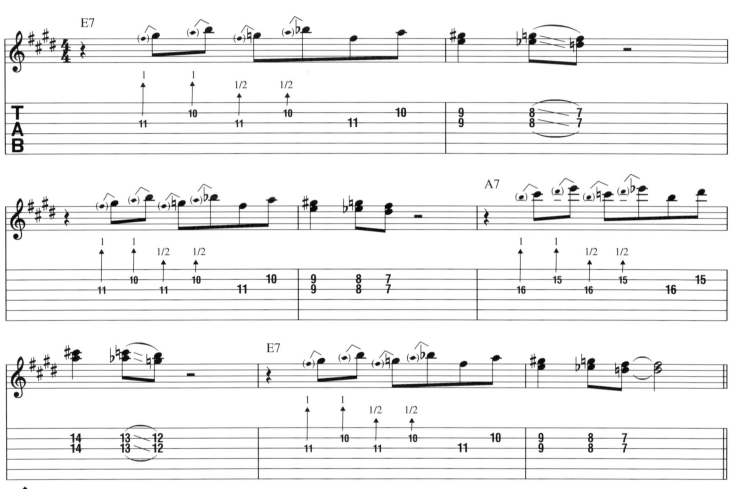

15 Pro Lick #15

Here's a pedal-steel tag which gets its sound by bending F♯ to G♯ on beat 1 and holding the bend through bar 1 until it is finally released at the end of bar 1.

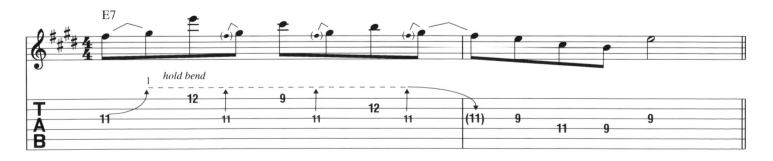

◆16 Pro Lick #16

Here is a lick over C7 using tricky double-stop bends. When bending two notes simultaneously, it seems to be easier if you imagine that the two fingers you are bending with are welded together and unable to move independently of one another. You then bend the notes, concentrating on bending your weakest finger in tune. Your strong finer will follow your weak finger and bend the other note automatically in tune. Try it, you'll see!

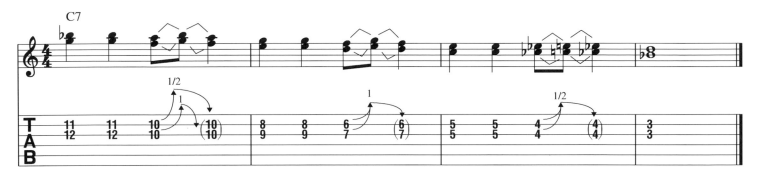

◆17 Pro Lick #17

This is a variation on the preceding lick—this time moving to either a I chord or a IV chord, depending on how you look at it.

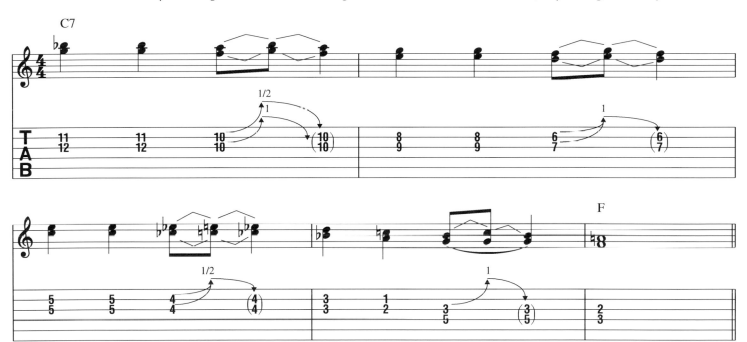

◆18 Pro Lick #18

This lick has a swing feel and works well in a western swing situation. The double-string half-note bends will probably need some practice.

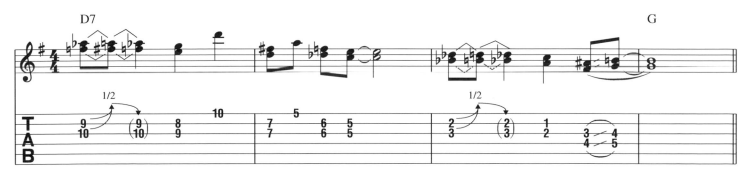

Open-String Licks

◆19 Pro Lick #19

This lick or tag in C utilizies several open strings which fall into the C scale. The lick is best played using an alternating motion between the pick and middle finger. Remember, in all open string licks, try to keep the left-hand fingers arched and perpendicular to the fingerboard so all surrounding strings are allowed to ring throughout the entire lick.

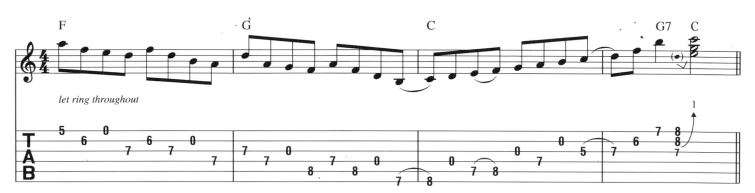

◆20 Pro Lick #20

This lick uses a descending half-step fingering with an open string to create a banjo style lick through a cycle of fourths chord progression.

◆21 Pro Lick #21

This blues or swing lick can also make a great ending (G7 to C). Pay close attention to the open strings.

◆22 Pro Lick #22

This one may be a bit tricky as it is meant to be played fast. It's a bluesy lick, and may be used in a variety of country and bluegrass situations.

◆23 Pro Lick #23

Here's a funky bluesy lick utilizing open strings. There are no special tricks—other than remembering to allow the open strings to ring throughout the entire lick.

Chord Licks

◆24 Pro Lick #24

This lick demonstrates the popular country sound of playing sixths over a typical chord change.

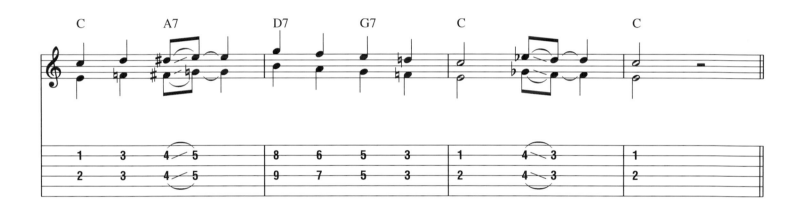

◆25 Pro Lick #25

The voicings in the first measure may take some stretching. Also, the use of a volume pedal can be helpful in achieving the steel guitar sound.

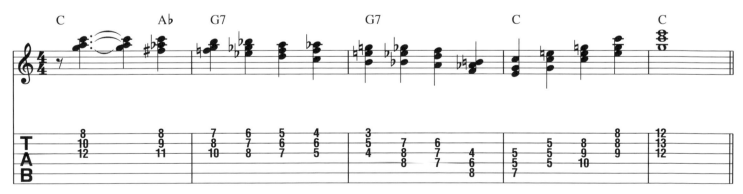

26 Pro Lick #26

This is a western swing-style chord melody phrase that makes a good introduction.

27 Pro Lick #27

This chord lick can be played over any dominant seventh chord (C7, V7) resolving to the tonic (F, I).

Rockabilly Licks

Most country gigs require the playing of fifties pop and rockabilly music. The phrases in this section will aid both country and rockabilly guitarists who need authentic rockabilly licks in their repertoire.

In the words of Carl Perkins, "Mix Fats Domino, Chuck Berry, and a little Bill Monroe and you've got rockabilly music." To be more specific, rockabilly was a fusion of country (then called "hillbilly" music), Chicago-style blues, and the then-prevalent swing sound.

For a goldmine of licks and phrases that can be applied to rockabilly, listen not only to early rockabilly guitarists such as Scotty Moore, Carl Perkins, and James Burton, but also go back and check out the recordings of Charlie Christian. In the early forties, Christian's blues-flavored eighth-note swing lines were a direct forerunner not only to rockabilly, but to bebop jazz as well.

 Pro Lick #28

This lick works great over G, G7, or Em as a lead lick or ending.

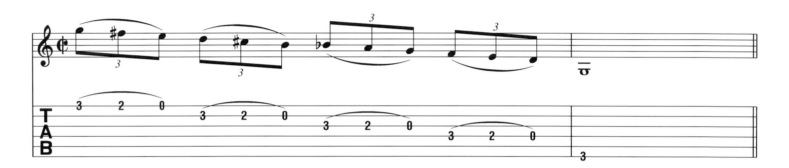

 Pro Lick #29

This well-known rockabilly lick ought to ring a bell!

◆30 Pro Lick #30

Here is another very popular blues or rockabilly lick.

◆31 Pro Lick #31

Note the use of the ♭3rd (G) in the first and third measures to get the "blues" sound.

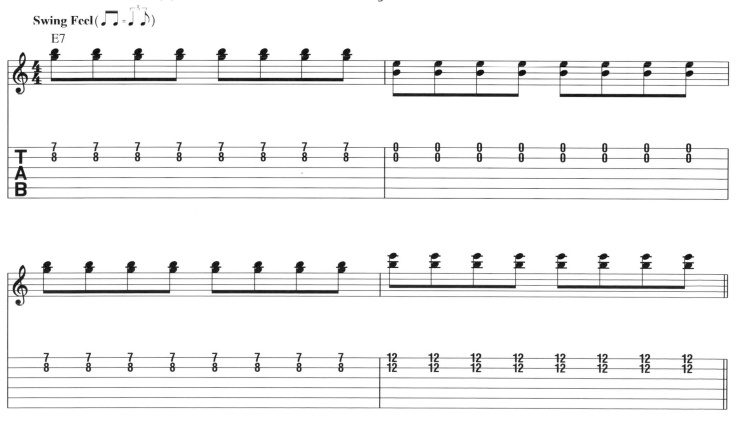

◆32 Pro Lick #32

This lick works best over a I (A7) or IV (D7) chord. Notice that the lick is repeated in the last two bars, phrased in triplets.

◆33 Pro Lick #33

This is an expanded version of lick #28. It's been used by everyone from Chet Atkins (who probably invented it) to the Stray Cats.

🔶34 Pro Lick #34

Here is a rockabilly blues chorus in C containing many of the classic licks of the style, such as: sliding into the double stops from a half-step below, repetitious rhythmic phrases, and a driving rhythm derived from playing mostly on the down beats.

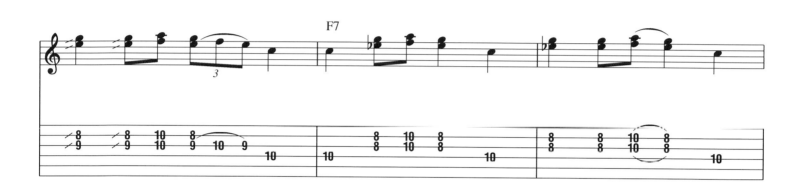

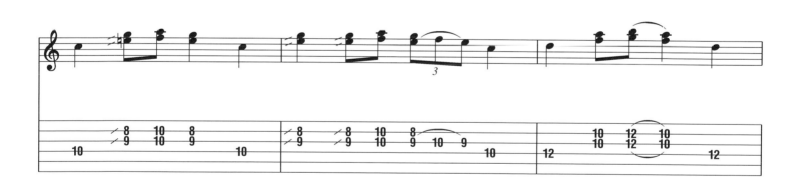

◆35◆ Pro Lick #35

This boogie tune reflects a bluegrass influence à la Doc Watson.

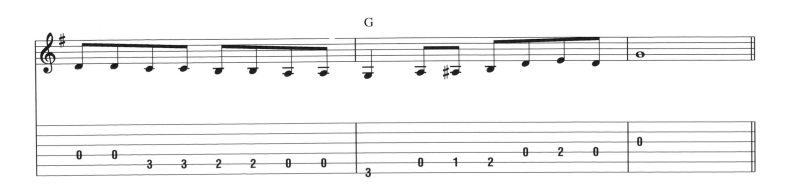

◆36 Pro Lick #36

This typical boogie lick can be played as a rhythm part or a really hot solo at faster tempos.

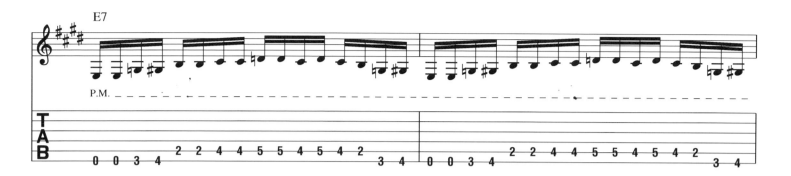

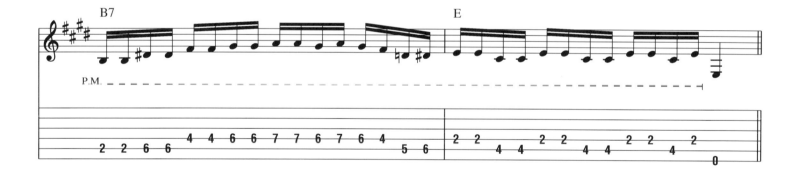

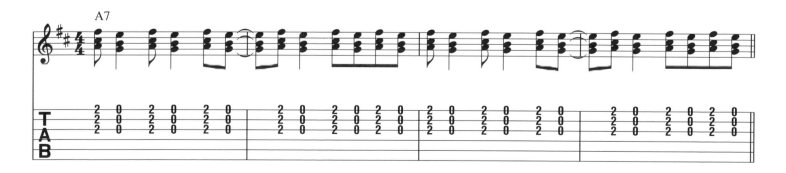

◆37 Pro Lick #37

This lick can be played using only one finger, but the timing is tricky. Try moving it up twelve frets (one octave) and play it over the same chord.

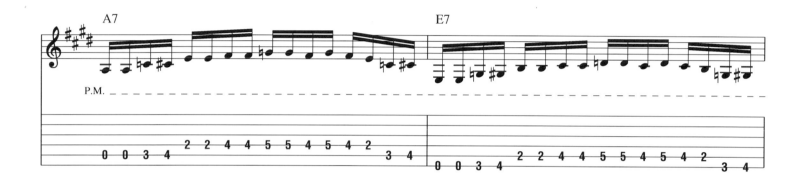

Funky Country Licks

38 Pro Lick #38

Here's a funky country lick that could also be played as a blues lick.

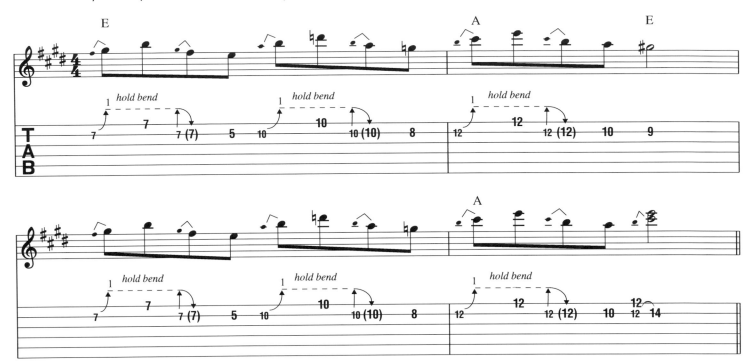

39 Pro Lick #39

Our lick for this typical chord progression depends on the bends and funky sound for its effect.

40 Pro Lick #40

This country blues lick can be played over A7 or D7.

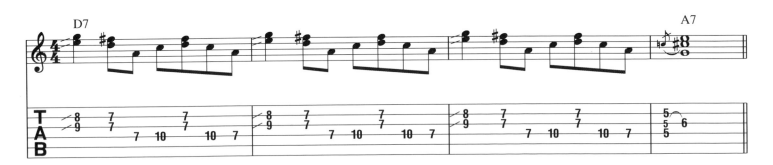

41 Pro Lick #41

This is one of our favorites and is actually a lot easier than it looks on paper. The X's indicate ghost or muffled notes which are achieved by not pressing the string all the way down to the fret, but just touching it with the left hand and picking it with the right hand so it sounds like a thump.

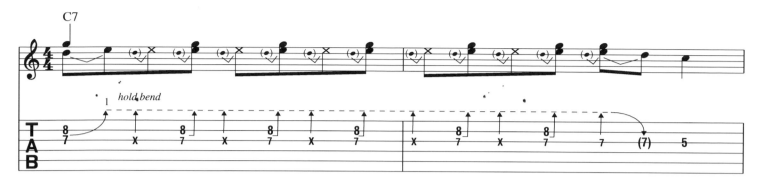

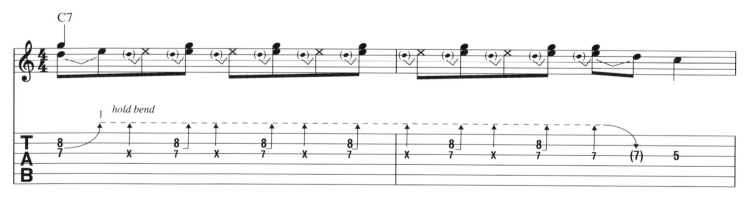

42 Pro Lick #42

Here's a variation of the preceding lick which again resolves to a I or IV chord depending on where you're coming from.

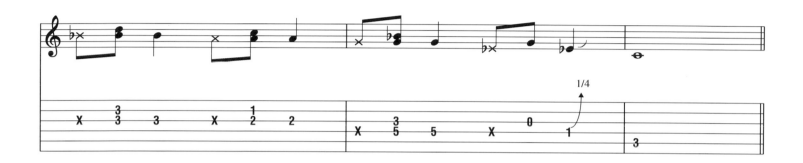

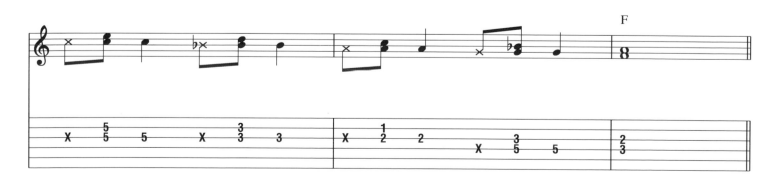

43 Pro Lick #43

Notice in this lick the pre-bends and release bends in beat 2 of bar 2 and beat 1 of bar 3. The first bend is accomplished by bending both notes up a half step using the first finger. The second is done by bending the C to D with the third finger while fretting F with the fourth finger.

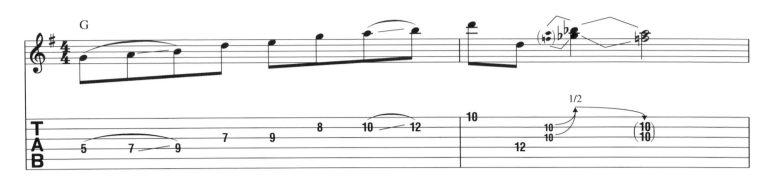

44 Pro Lick #44

This is a great four-bar funky lick which employs effective use of both the pentatonic and blues scales with a shift from fifth to second position in bar 3.

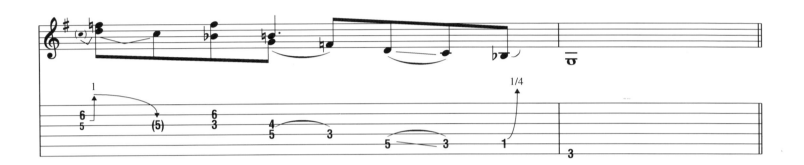

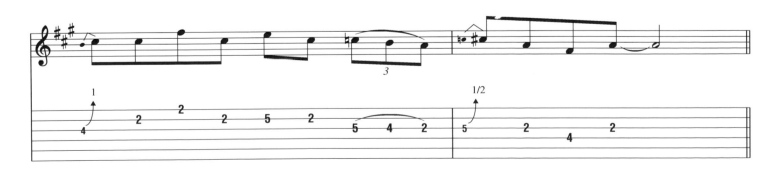

◆45 Pro Lick #45

Here's a three-bar funky lick, any bar of which may be used as a lick in itself.

◆46 Pro Lick #46

In this up-tempo blues chorus in A, bars 13-16 contain a funky lick reminiscent of early Jerry Reed.

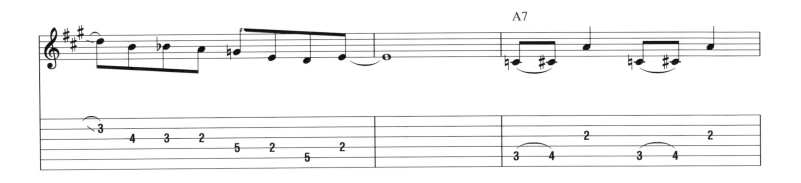

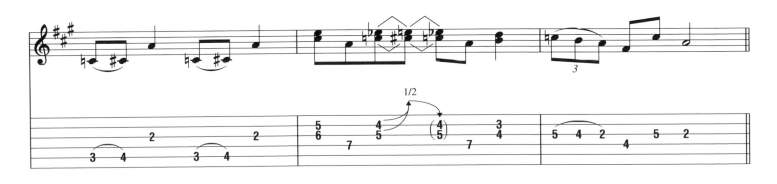

47 Pro Lick #47

The bends in this lick create an earthy pedal-steel sound. Be sure to bend in tune and watch the timing.

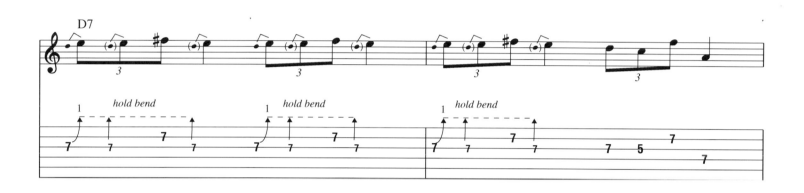

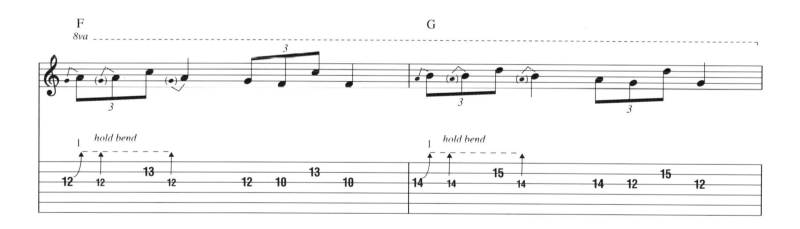

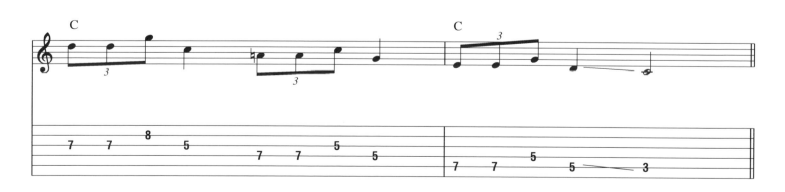

◆48 Pro Lick #48

This is a piano-style lick that is great for lead or backup, especially in the bluesy country vein.

◆49 Pro Lick #49

Here is another piano-style boogie lick which could be used as a rhythm part or a lead lick.

◆50 Pro Lick #50

The use of double stops, bends, and blue notes gives this lick its funky sound. Be careful of the pre-bends in bar 1, beat 3, and in bar 2, beat 1.

◆51 Pro Lick #51

This V–IV–V–I lick shows a definite British rock influence, but the phrasing makes it country all the way.

◆52 Pro Lick #52

Although this lick looks difficult on paper, practice it slowly and the speed will come later.

◆53 Pro Lick #53

Watch for the pull-offs, hammer-ons, and slides in this bluesy country lick.

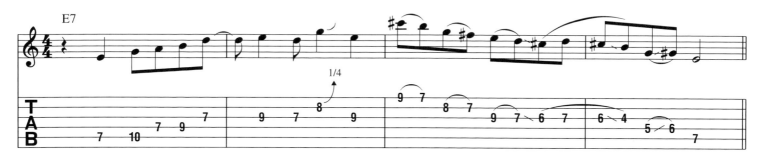

◆54 Pro Lick #54

In playing this funky lick, it is necessary to use right-hand fingers as well as a pick because of wide interval skips. Try playing the open A string with your pick and the double stops with your fingers. This method is not only more precise, but it will give the lick more snap.

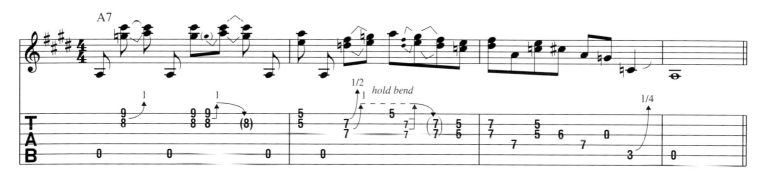

◆55 Pro Lick #55

This is one of the most satisfying licks to play once it is mastered. It is extremely funky à la Jerry Reed or Albert Lee. Pay close attention to fingers and be careful of prebends in bar 1. Also, be sure to bend the notes to exact pitch before playing.

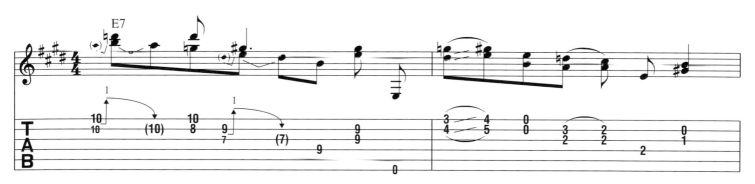

Guitar Notation Legend

Guitar Music can be notated three different ways: on a *musical staff*, in *tablature*, and in *rhythm slashes*.

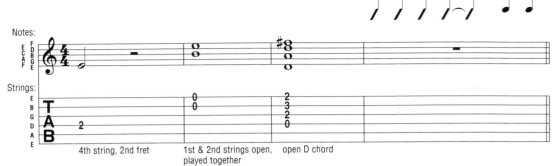

RHYTHM SLASHES are written above the staff. Strum chords in the rhythm indicated. Use the chord diagrams found at the top of the first page of the transcription for the appropriate chord voicings. Round noteheads indicate single notes.

THE MUSICAL STAFF shows pitches and rhythms and is divided by bar lines into measures. Pitches are named after the first seven letters of the alphabet.

TABLATURE graphically represents the guitar fingerboard. Each horizontal line represents a string, and each number represents a fret.

4th string, 2nd fret   1st & 2nd strings open, played together   open D chord

HALF-STEP BEND: Strike the note and bend up 1/2 step.

WHOLE-STEP BEND: Strike the note and bend up one step.

GRACE NOTE BEND: Strike the note and bend up as indicated. The first note does not take up any time.

SLIGHT (MICROTONE) BEND: Strike the note and bend up 1/4 step.

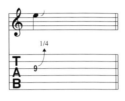

BEND AND RELEASE: Strike the note and bend up as indicated, then release back to the original note. Only the first note is struck.

PRE-BEND: Bend the note as indicated, then strike it.

VIBRATO: The string is vibrated by rapidly bending and releasing the note with the fretting hand.

WIDE VIBRATO: The pitch is varied to a greater degree by vibrating with the fretting hand.

HAMMER-ON: Strike the first (lower) note with one finger, then sound the higher note (on the same string) with another finger by fretting it without picking.

PULL-OFF: Place both fingers on the notes to be sounded. Strike the first note and without picking, pull the finger off to sound the second (lower) note.

LEGATO SLIDE: Strike the first note and then slide the same fret-hand finger up or down to the second note. The second note is not struck.

SHIFT SLIDE: Same as legato slide, except the second note is struck.

TRILL: Very rapidly alternate between the notes indicated by continuously hammering on and pulling off.

TAPPING: Hammer ("tap") the fret indicated with the pick-hand index or middle finger and pull off to the note fretted by the fret hand.

NATURAL HARMONIC: Strike the note while the fret-hand lightly touches the string directly over the fret indicated.

PINCH HARMONIC: The note is fretted normally and a harmonic is produced by adding the edge of the thumb or the tip of the index finger of the pick hand to the normal pick attack.

PICK SCRAPE: The edge of the pick is rubbed down (or up) the string, producing a scratchy sound.

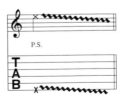

MUFFLED STRINGS: A percussive sound is produced by laying the fret hand across the string(s) without depressing, and striking them with the pick hand.

PALM MUTING: The note is partially muted by the pick hand lightly touching the string(s) just before the bridge.

RAKE: Drag the pick across the strings indicated with a single motion.

TREMOLO PICKING: The note is picked as rapidly and continuously as possible.

VIBRATO BAR DIVE AND RETURN: The pitch of the note or chord is dropped a specified number of steps (in rhythm) then returned to the original pitch.

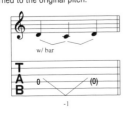

VIBRATO BAR SCOOP: Depress the bar just before striking the note, then quickly release the bar.

VIBRATO BAR DIP: Strike the note and then immediately drop a specified number of steps, then release back to the original pitch.